NATIONAL GEOGRAPHIC OUR WORLD

The TUG-of-WAR

A Folktale from Africa

Retold by Leo Fletcher

NATIONAL GEOGRAPHIC LEARNING | CENGAGE Learning

Every morning, a group of jungle animals gathered at the local watering hole to talk, drink, and tell stories.

One hot morning, Lion joined the group. He was very excited. He had amazing news.

"I just saw Elephant push over a giant tree!" said Lion. "Elephant is the strongest animal in the jungle."

Not everyone agreed with Lion.

"I disagree," said Zebra a little carefully. (Zebra was always nervous around Lion.) "Yesterday, I saw Hippo push a big boat with her nose! She's stronger."

The other animals joined the conversation, which soon became an argument.

"Elephant is stronger!" said Lion, Ostrich, and Snake.

"No. Hippo is!" said Zebra, Monkey, and Giraffe.

Finally, someone said, "Elephant and Hippo aren't so strong. I'm as strong as they are!"

The animals all turned to see who spoke. It was Turtle!

"You're as strong as Elephant and Hippo?" said the other animals. "Ha ha ha!"

The more Turtle talked about his strength, the more the animals laughed.

Finally, Turtle said, "Okay. I'll prove it."

Then Turtle walked into the jungle.

Turtle found Elephant.

"Hey!" said Turtle. "I bet I can beat you in a game of tug-of-war!"

Turtle gave Elephant the end of a long vine.

"Hold this," said Turtle. "When you feel me pull on it, you start to pull."

Then Turtle walked into the jungle.

Turtle took the other end of the vine to the other side of the jungle. He found Hippo.

"Hey, Hippo!" said Turtle. "I bet I can beat you in a game of tug-of-war!"

Turtle gave the other end of the vine to Hippo and told her what to do.

Turtle said, "When I pull, you pull! OK?"

Deep in the jungle, Turtle grabbed the middle of the vine.

"Elephant and Hippo can't see me," said Turtle. "And they can't see each other. Now I can have some fun!"

Turtle tugged the vine.

Elephant felt the tug and started to pull on his end.

Hippo felt it, too, and pulled on her end.

Elephant and Hippo pulled on the vine for hours. The more Elephant pulled, the more Hippo pulled. No one was winning. They didn't move forward or backward. They just pulled.

"Wow!" thought Elephant. "Turtle IS strong."

"Wow!" thought Hippo. "Turtle is SO strong!"

Turtle just sat, watched the vine, and laughed.

Finally, Elephant and Hippo gave the vine one last big tug.
They pulled with such force that the vine snapped!
Elephant fell over with a THUD!
Hippo fell over with a SPLASH!
Turtle just watched and laughed.

SNAP!

The next morning, the animals talked excitedly.
"Did you hear about Turtle?" said Lion.
"Yes!" said Giraffe. "He's as strong as Elephant and as strong as Hippo!"
"They couldn't beat him in a tug-of-war!" said Ostrich.
Turtle was nearby and heard them.
"I'm not as strong as the other animals," said Turtle. "But I'm a lot smarter!"

Facts About Force

Think of how many times you push or pull things in a day. For example, maybe you push your little sister on a swing or pull a suitcase on wheels.

push

pull

Push and Pull

When you push and pull things, you use **force**. Force moves something forward or backward. When something moves, it is called **motion**. Force causes motion.

push

pull

12

Tug-of-War

In the game of tug-of-war, the force is pulling. Two teams pull on the ends of a rope. If the two teams are the same size and have the same strength, then no motion happens.

pull

The same thing can happen with pushing. If two people (or animals) of the same weight and strength push against each other, neither will move. The forces are balanced.

push

In a game of tug-of-war, if one team has more or stronger people, that team usually can pull the other team forward. The losing team falls forward. And the bigger, stronger team usually wins.

Fun with Force

What's happening in the picture? Write a sentence about each number. Use one word from the box in each sentence.

backward	forward	push	pull	fall over

1 He is pushing the girl.

2 _____

3 _____

4 _____

5 _____

Which force is used in each picture? Write **push** or **pull**.

1. _push_

2. _____

3. _____

4. _____

5. _____

6. _____

What are things you pull? What are things you push? Write a list of as many things as you can think of. Use a bilingual dictionary if necessary.

Glossary

agreed thought the same thing as someone else

argument

argument a fight with words when people do not agree

conversation a talk

excited filled with a strong feeling

joined became a part of

jungle a hot area with many trees and plants

jungle

nervous worried that something bad is going to happen

snap to break suddenly with a sharp, cracking sound

tugged pulled

tug-of-war a game in which two teams pull on opposite ends of a rope to try to move each other

watering hole

vine a long part of some plants that looks like a rope

watering hole a hole with water in it where wild animals go to drink